acknowledgements

My appreciation goes to these very special designers who embraced my vision for this title and created the unique, innovative and inspiring projects in this book. To Mary Ann Donze, Donna Martin, Diane McCauley, Tamara Vandergriff and Marge Wooters, thank-you for your dedication. A particular thanks to Secely Palmer for coordinating the production process. The creative journey can be as challenging as it is rewarding and a lot of fun.

To Jan Carr and his team at Clover Needlecraft who continuously introduce superior new products to the fabric and needle arts market, I thank you for your partnership and support for this title and for **Needle Felted Accessories**.

©2007 Amy Barickman, Indygo Junction Inc.

Published by Indygo Junction
P.O. Box 30238
Kansas City , MO 64112

913-341-5559
www.indygojunction.com

ISBN-10 0-9754918-0-6
ISBN-13 978-09754918-0-5

We take great care to ensure that the information included in our patterns is accurate and presented in good faith. No warranty is provided nor results guaranteed. For your convenience, we post an up-to-date listing of corrections on our website www.indygojunction.com. If a correction is not noted, please contact our customer service department at info@indygojunction.com or 913-341-5559. You may also write us at PO Box 30238, Kansas City, MO 64112.

Needle Felted Fashions

Amy Barickman

DESIGNER CREDITS:

Mary Ann Donze
Collage Sweater
Baby Bouquet Sweater and Hat
Swirl Girl Child's Coat

Donna Martin
Ascot Scarf
Floral Fleece Scarf

Diane McCauley
Diamonds on Parade
Art Nouveau Jacket

Tamara Vandergriff
Tulip Poncho

Marge Wooters
Flower Vine Jeans

About the Author

Amy Barickman is a leader in the quilt and clothing pattern craft industry. After graduating from Kansas University with a degree in art and design, she founded Indygo Junction in 1990 to publish and market patterns designed by fresh, new talent. Amy's knack for anticipating popular trends has led her to discover artists and guide them to create with innovative materials.

As technology improved she envisioned what crafters might accomplish with their home computer and printer. She founded The Vintage Workshop in 2002 to create products that combine timeless vintage artwork with the computer and inkjet printable materials using downloads from her website and CDs.

To date Amy has identified and marketed more than 25 designers and published 600 pattern titles and 70 books, including *Needle Felted Fashions*. She inspires countless crafters to open their own creative spirit and experiment with the newest sewing, fabric and crafting technologies.

Indygo Junction is a leader in the development of designs and techniques for the art of needle felting. Our first book *Indygo Junction's Needle Felting, 22 Stylish Projects for Home and Fashion*, published by C&T Publishing, was an instant best-seller. The techniques offer unlimited creative applications, and now we bring additional patterns and technical know-how in this book, *Needle Felted Fashions,* with a collection of 10 designs. A third book, *Needle Felted Accessories,* includes jewelry-making techniques.

Tools

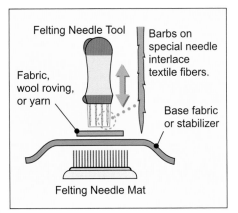

Projects featured in this book have been created with *Clover's Felting Needle Tool, Felting Needle Mat* and *Wool Roving Fiber.* The felting needles have barbs that allow fibers to mesh and interlock using just a light touch to punch. This multi-needle tool will make needling comfortable and effortless with the spring action it provides. As the needles are VERY sharp, this tool offers a locking safety cover.

We also suggest using a single needle for some projects. When using a single needle, take extra care not to stab too deeply, only 1/2" or so. If you stab too deeply, you run the risk of breaking the needle on the base of the mat.

The tool <u>must</u> be used with the *Felting Needle Mat*, which is available in 2 sizes – small and large. We prefer the large mat because it covers more surface area when you work on the project, but the small mat works well for felting in tight spaces – like embellishing the sleeve of a sweater or the leg of a jean pant. The brush allows the needles to move easily thru materials you are felting and protects needles from breaking or dulling. Unlike using a foam block, this brush mat does not wear out or breakdown.

We recommend both Clover's fine and heavy gauge needles. The majority of the projects have been created using heavy 38-gauge multi-purpose needles. For finer details use the 40-gauge needle. The tool comes with 5 fine needles. Replacement needles are sold separately.

In recent years, there are new machines available dedicated specifically to needle felting, as well as needle felting tool attachments for sewing machines. These machines will felt aggressively. We find the Clover tool works well to baste a design in place before felting with a machine.

Fibers, Fabrics, and Yarns

When choosing material to needle felt, we suggest wool or natural fibers. Projects in this book feature roving (carded and combed wool before it is spun), yarn, and fabric appliqués (wool, cotton and silk). When determining fabrics that can be used for felting, we suggest testing materials first to see if you achieve your desired results and understand the care that will be required, whether it is felting a fiber to fabric or a fabric to fabric combination.

The roving fiber featured in this book is Clover Needlecraft brand. It is available individually (0.7 ounces) as well as in assortment packs. The natural sheep's wool roving is exported from Australia and dyed in Japan.

Methods for creating designs in fiber

Projects in *Needle Felted Fashions* use several methods, including one for a non-woven, water-soluble stabilizer. This material works very well as a foundation for creating a fiber design, and then easily can be washed away before or after the design is affixed to the base fabric. Because this material is translucent, pattern designs can be easily traced on to the material. The *Tulip Poncho* and *Flower Vine Jeans* explain the processes.

Creating a design using non-woven, water-soluble stabilizer.

Needle felting a wool appliqué.

We also feature designs that use wool appliqués needled into a base fabric. Felted wool will work best for this method, as raw edges will not ravel. To felt your woven and knitted woolens (to make them dense), start by washing them in warm water and drying on low heat. Repeat this process to achieve desired thickness. Shrinkage will vary by machine (top or front loading) and the wool material you are felting. Remember to test your materials when using appliqués, because all wools react differently. The density of the weave in wool fiber will come into play when one material is bonded to another. Remember you don't have to stick with what others have done. Experiment!

diamonds on parade

Have an unlined wool jacket in the back of your closet that needs some pizzazz? Or, pick up a new or gently used jacket from a thrift store and make it your own. This simple argyle pattern can be adapted to just about any style or type of jacket.

Materials

- Unlined wool jacket (boiled wool jackets, as pictured, work well)
- Small scraps of coordinating wools (one or more colors, either solids or patterns)
- Wool worsted-weight yarn in a coordinating color (solid or variegated)
- Sewing pins
- Clover felting needle tool and/or single felting needles
- Clover felting needle mat
- Diamond pattern pieces for the large and small diamonds (located in Pattern Insert)

An argyle pattern is a very simple arrangement of diamonds placed point to point. These will be cut from one or more colors of wool and applied to the jacket. To complete the pattern, wool yarn is used to add a pattern of diamonds atop the wool.

Construction:

1. Analyze the style of the jacket that you plan to use. Decide where the embellishment would look best on your particular jacket. It may be a construction detail such as a front or a back yoke, a back panel or the collar. Or, if the jacket is lacking in details, simply decide where you think the embellishment would look best – the upper back, down the length of the sleeve, on the center front, etc. You also have the option of needle felting yarn to simulate a construction detail. For example, your jacket has a one-piece back, but you would like to add a yoke detail. Mark where you would like the appearance of a yoke, and needle felt a segment of yarn along the mark.

2. Cut a number of diamonds from plain or colored scrap paper. Arrange them on the jacket to test how many wool diamonds you will need and how the pattern will work on your particular size jacket. The diamonds can be arranged horizontally or vertically, all one size or a mix.

If the diamonds don't quite fit the area you want to embellish, you can either reduce or enlarge the diamonds until the number that you wish to use will fit. Or, you can modify one or more diamonds to fill the area.

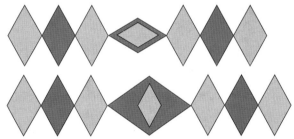

3. When satisfied with the pattern, cut the diamonds from the wool scraps. Use a chalk marker to mark guidelines for placement. Arrange the diamonds on the jacket and pin in place. Needle felt securely in place. If desired, layer a smaller diamond in a contrasting color on one or more large diamonds and needle felt in place.

4. Mark a line with the chalk marker midway between the center point of each diamond and the top and bottom (or the distance you desire.)

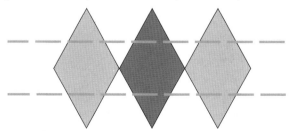

diamonds on parade continued

continued

Tip: Use a sewing pin to help you position the yarn. Needle felt the first line segment. Place a pin where the yarn is to change direction. Pull the yarn around the pin and lay the pin flat on the fabric with the point through the jacket fabric. Hold the yarn in place and lightly needle felt the next segment. You can lightly needle felt directly over the pin to anchor the yarn, then remove the pin and continue needle felting to secure.

6. Cut a second length of yarn and repeat to complete the argyle pattern.

7. If desired, add additional yarn detailing. The brown jacket pictured has large (approximately 3/8") running stitches worked by hand using the worsted weight yarn near the edge of the collar and cuffs.

5. Cut a generous length of yarn. Begin needle felting the yarn in a series of diagonals, with the points on the marked line and directly above where the wool diamonds meet.

collage sweater

A crewneck (or turtleneck) sweater gives its life for art as it is deconstructed to create a one-of-a-kind embellished V-neck sweater with three-quarter sleeves. Use scraps, strips and snippets of "can't throw it away" fabric to reassemble in an artistic fashion. Begin with a 100% wool sweater a bit larger than you normally wear to create a sweater with more of a tunic fit.

Materials

- One adult 100% wool sweater slightly larger than your regular size. A crewneck or turtleneck will work. The sample was constructed from a man's dark moss green turtleneck.

- Three colors of Clover natural wool roving (sample uses brown, rust and moss green)

- An assortment of beads (sample uses mainly brown, dark rose and green hues)

- An assortment of fabric scraps (sample uses patterned wools, recycled menswear woolens, silk, Japanese cottons, vintage barkcloth, cotton velvet, vintage brocade, pre-felted wool and tie-dyed wool) Select an odd mix of textures, sheen and color fields.

Materials *continued*

- Embroidery floss in several colors (sample uses orange, burgundy, turquoise, lavender, brown and green)
- Sewing thread (sample uses gold)
- Clover felting needle tool and/or single felting needles. A multi-needle tool is suggested.
- Clover felting needle mat or sturdy piece of foam on which to felt. A larger piece of very dense foam to fit under sweater front when arranging collage is helpful but not essential.
- A liquid product to prevent fraying

Felting Instructions:

Wash your sweater in warm water and dry on low heat. This will significantly shrink your sweater and condense the fibers so that it no longer ravels when cut. Sometimes it is necessary to repeat this procedure to achieve the desired "density". The condensed fibers make a good palate for felting in wool roving and other fibers. Don't felt too much or your wool will become too stiff to wear comfortably.

Cutting Instructions:

1. Try on sweater and let the arms hang straight down. Mark the point at which you desire your three quarter length sleeves to fall. Remove sweater and cut straight across at this point, parallel with sleeve bottom edges. Set aside lower sleeves.

2. Remove the crew-neck or turtleneck ribbing by carefully cutting around lower edge. Discard.

3. Locate the center of the neck front. Determine how deep you would like your V neck and move straight down from neck center to this point. Mark. Using illustration as a guide, cut from neck to this point on both sides.

4. Notes on cutting shapes for collage: It is helpful to have a stack of potential fabric scraps next to you. Begin by cutting many scraps into various shapes and sizes to get you started. You may or may not use them all but by placing them on sweater initially you can see what needs to be added, subtracted or altered. When cutting shapes, do not use a straight edge. It is more interesting if they are cut free hand. Make some more organic in shape with one curved side, etc. Cut some with pinking shears if desired. Cut a variety of sizes – some long and thin, some more substantial rectangles and small squares. Our sample also features five leaf shapes. One cotton velvet and two silk leaves that are about 2" long. Two are also cut from pre-felted wool and are 1 5/8" and 2 1/4" long. These are a few of the dimensions we used just to give you an idea of how to start: 4" x 2", 6" x 2 1/2", 8" x 1", 1" x 3", 3 1/2" x 5/8".

collage sweater

NONE are perfect rectangles or squares. Let them be wider at one end or pointed or curved. The sample also has a pre-felted wool circle that is 1 3/4" diameter with a bit of wool roving felted in the center.

Embellishment Instructions:

1. Place felting mat inside lower sleeve at edge. Pull out a long section of brown roving and begin felting into the very edge of cut sleeve. Continue all around, adding roving until the cut sleeve edge is sufficiently stabilized to prevent raveling, approximately 3/8" wide. Just above this brown roving, felt rust roving in the same manner all around lower sleeve approximately 1/4" wide. Apply roving liberally. Repeat on remaining sleeve.

2. Place felting mat under the cut V-neck edge. As you did on the sleeves, you will stabilize the cut edge by felting in brown roving all around the neck, approximately 3/8" wide. Just below the brown roving, felt in rust roving as well, approximately 1/4" wide. Apply roving liberally.

3. Now to create your collage. Use photograph as a guideline but create your own. Have it vaguely follow that V shape of the neck. If you have a large piece of foam, slide it under sweater front. Start arranging fabric, preferably with any wool pieces on the bottom. Tack in place with a felting needle. Once you have a base layer you like, felt in securely with the multi-needle tool. Now layer additional fabrics on top such as cottons, silks and brocades. You can felt these in to a certain extent but they will need additional decorative stitching to remain secure.

4. Use a variety of embroidery floss colors (two to three strands at a time) to make parallel lines of running stitches through these fabric pieces. Make some horizontal, some vertical and some diagonal. On some you may just stitch around the perimeter. In a couple of areas a single strand of sewing thread was used for a more delicate look.

5. When you have completed application of fabric, add some wisps of wool roving. The sample uses all moss green in long slightly curved arcs of varying length. It should easily felt in to your sweater and over any fabrics. You may also use your wool roving to create small spiral shapes randomly throughout your collage or to make veins on your leaves.

6. The last step of embellishing is adding your beads. Stitch them on singly or in clusters. Line one side of a leaf or cover an entire shape. By applying them throughout the collage, the piece is unified visually.

7. After you are satisfied with your collage, use your liquid anti-fraying product to LIGHTLY go around the edges of your non-wool fabrics.

NOTE: We did not do this on sample but you can use the lower sleeves you removed to make front patch pockets for sweater. Open out and turn so that ribbing is up. Cut to desired width. Pin on pocket front and hand stitch around perimeter with embroidery floss or machine stitch to garment.

flower vine jeans

Using our unique method, this design can be customized to fit your wardrobe — jeans or a denim jacket.

Materials

- 1 pair of denim jeans
- Clover natural wool roving in the following colors: (Numbers reference the location of the roving color on the Flower Vine Design, which is provided in the Pattern Insert.) 1-red, 2-rust, 3-gold, 4-moss green, 5-orange, 6-brown, 7-violet

- Crewel wool yarn for stems, leaf veins and outlining of flowers, etc. in the following colors: (Letters reference the location of the yarn color outlining on the Flower Vine Design, which is provided in the Pattern Insert.) A-red, B-rust, C-green, D-black, E-brown
- Silk ribbon in brown (optional)

Materials *continued*

- Small seed beads for sparkle on flowers in iridescent white and iridescent violet
- Non-Woven Water Soluble Stabilizer
- Pen or pencil
- Flower Vine Design (provided in Pattern Insert)
- Clover felting needle tool and/or single felting needles
- Clover felting needle mat

Needle Felting Instructions:

1. Trace designs onto stabilizer using pencil or pen. Trace only the flowers and leaves. The stems will be done when attached to the jeans.

2. Needle Felt designs onto the stabilizer using the roving colors on the pattern. Coverage should be thick enough not to see any of the stabilizer showing through. To make shaping easier, trim roving pieces to match curves and points on the design and then needle felt. Use the crewel yarn around the edges, etc.

3. When the design is complete, trim away the stabilizer close to the needle felting being careful not to cut the needle felting.

Assembly Instructions:

1. Place each needle felted piece on jeans as in finished design (use pins to secure), cutting flowers and leaves apart as necessary.

2. When satisfied with design placement, carefully needle felt each piece to the jeans by placing the felting needle mat inside jeans underneath each felted piece and gently needle felt until piece is secure. Check the back side to be sure fibers are coming through.

3. Continue this procedure until all flowers and leaves are in place.

4. Place the brown crewel yarn for the stems. Needle felt in place. If desired the silk ribbon can be added to the top of the brown yarn for an additional texture.

5. Add beads to flower centers and petal edges.

6. Jeans are machine washable. We recommend turning inside out and washing on the gentle cycle, in cold water. Dry on low heat setting. (This will remove excess stabilizer.)

Note: The top flower on the front pocket is felted through the pocket lining. Be sure to move the pocket lining out of the way for the remaining flowers or you won't be able to use the pocket.

tulip poncho

A design, Scandinavian in style, adorns this easy-to-sew wool poncho created from two rectangular pieces of fabric.

Materials

- 1 yd. of black wool (any width)
- Matching thread
- Clover natural wool roving in the following colors: (Numbers reference the location of the roving color on the Tulip Design that is provided in the Pattern Insert.) 1-lime green, 2-moss green, 3-blue, 4-teal, 5-violet, 6-orange

- Yarn for flower stems (teal)
- Non-Woven Water Soluble Stabilizer
- Low tack painter's tape
- Tulip Design (provided in Pattern Insert)
- Clover felting needle tool and/or single felting needles. A multi-needle tool is suggested.
- Clover felting needle mat

Cutting Instructions:
Cut 2 pieces of wool 32" x 16"

Needle Felting Instructions:

1. Trace design onto non-woven water soluble stabilizer using pencil or pen. Leaving about a 2" border around the entire design, roughly cut design out.

2. Using painters tape, attach the cut out design to the lower left hand corner (with fabric laying horizontal) of the right side of one of the pieces of wool; 4 1/2" from the bottom short edge and 2" from the long side edge. See diagram to right.

3. Needle felt design through the stabilizer onto the piece of wool using the roving colors on the pattern. Coverage should be thick enough not to see any of the black wool showing through. To make shaping easier, trim roving pieces to match curves and points

on the design and then needle felt. Very thin pieces of rolled roving can be used for the flower stems or yarn may be substituted.

4. When the design is complete, trim away the stabilizer as close as possible to the needle felted design, being careful not to cut either the wool or the design.

5. Very lightly spritz the needle felted design with water to dissolve the stabilizer. Use a cotton swab to gently rub off any remaining stabilizer. Use a paper towel to blot up any excess water and stabilizer. Let dry.

Assembly Instructions:

1. Lay felted piece horizontally with the design in the lower left corner with right side up. Lay the blank piece of fabric right side down and place side E perpendicular over upper left corner of the felted piece (corner where A and B inter-

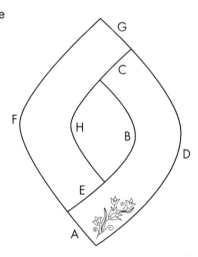

sect) so it forms a right angle. Be sure edges are even. Starting at the left upper corner stitch side E to side B allowing a 1/2" seam allowance. Stop 1/2" before end and backstitch.

2. With right sides together, stitch side C at a right angel to the corner where H and G intersect, making sure edges are even using 1/2" seam allowance. Stop 1/2" before end and backstitch.

3. On wrong side, press under a 1/2" hem on all raw edges (including top neck and bottom edge) and top stitch either by hand or machine.

ascot scarf

Scarf A

Combine yarns and roving to create your own unique fiber collage. There are endless possibilities for this easy no-sew accessory!

Materials

- 1/4 yard of natural colored wool felt (samples use National Nonwoven Woolfelt®)
- Clover natural wool roving colors:

  Scarf A: orange, lime green, orange, teal, violet, and moss green

  Scarf B: orange, lime green, teal, and moss green

  Scarf C: violet, pink, black and lime green

- For Scarf B only, you will need an assortment of wool yarns (to match your chosen color scheme)
- Clover felting needle tool and/or single felting needles. A multi-needle tool is suggested.
- Clover felting needle mat
- Optional – Invisible or matching thread to match wool felt

Cutting Instructions (all scarves):

Cut a piece of wool felt that measures 5 1/2" x 36"

Needle Felting Instructions:

Scarf A:

1. Randomly embellish with a variety of wool yarns and long wisps of wool roving in various colors and lay on top of wool felt per photograph or use your own imagination. Tack in place first, until you have the design you are pleased with, then needle felt in place.

Scarf B (shown on cover of book):

1. Take long pieces of lime green and orange wool roving and lay on top of wool felt in long stripes, parallel with the long edge of the scarf. The lime green stripe is located 1" from raw edge and the orange stripe is located 1" from the lime green stripe. See cover photograph. Tack in place with single needle.

2. Take long pieces of teal, violet, and moss green wool roving and lay on top of wool felt in long stripes, parallel with the short edge of the scarf (perpendicular to the first stripes in previous step). The teal stripe is located 2" from raw edge, the violet stripe is located 2" from the teal stripe, and the moss green stripe is located 2" from the violet stripe. See cover photograph. Tack in place with single needle.

3. You may want to weave the vertical and horizontal stripes to create a subtle plaid pattern. See cover photograph. Once you are happy with the layout, felt in place with multi-needle tool.

Scarf C:

1. Take long pieces of lime green, black, and pink wool roving and lay on top of wool felt in long stripes, parallel and equally spaced with the long edge of the scarf. Locate stripes 1" from both long

edges and 1 1/2" from each other. See photograph. Tack in place with single needle.

2. Take long pieces of violet, pink, black and lime green wool roving and lay on top of wool felt in long stripes, parallel and equally spaced with the short edge of the scarf (perpendicular to the first stripes in Step 1). Locate stripes approximately 3" from each other. See photograph. Tack in place with single needle. Next, follow Step 3 under Scarf B.

Assembly Instructions (all scarves):

1. Once you have your final design securely needle felted in place on your piece of wool felt. Wash in machine with other like colored clothes. Lay flat to dry; this may take over night to dry. While it is drying you can gently pull and stretch wool felt to desired look.

2. Once it is completely dry, cut a 3" slit lengthwise, parallel with long edge; centered and starting 3" from short end.

3. Needle felt around this 3" slit. Optional: Stitch around slit with invisible or matching thread to prevent stretching.

4. Optional: With scissors, trim corners round and cut a slight scallop pattern at long edges.

Scarf C

floral fleece scarf

A simple yet dramatic fashion statement needle felted on polar fleece. An easy design to embellish on a variety of garments.

Materials

- 1/3 yard black Polarfleece or Polartec®
- Clover natural wool roving in the following colors: (Numbers reference the location of the roving color on the Floral Fleece Scarf Design; that is provided in the Pattern Insert.) 1-pink, 2-violet, 3-teal, 4-moss green
- Water soluble marking pencil (optional)
- Saral tracing paper (optional)
- Floral Fleece Scarf Design (provided in Pattern Insert)
- Clover felting needle tool and/or single felting needles
- Clover felting needle mat

Cutting Instructions:

Cut 1 piece of fleece 60" long x 8" wide

Transfer the Design:

1. If you are comfortable with a free form approach, use the marking pencil to draw the Floral Fleece Design directly on your scarf. The larger flower design will be located at each end of your scarf. See photograph. Using the smaller flower/vine design and connecting it to the large flower design, repeat this smaller flower design so that one vine is longer than the vine at the opposite end, leaving about 14" of open space between to the two vines.

2. If you want more guidance for the pattern, use the Saral tracing paper per the manufacturer's directions and trace the design directly on to the fleece.

Needle Felting Instructions:

1. Beginning at one end of the scarf, needle felt the flowers, leaves and vines using wisps of wool roving. Shape the flowers, remembering that this process is very forgiving. If not correct, lift up and reshape. For vines roll long wisps of roving together on a wooden cutting board and add a little water to help bind roving together. Wisps of roving gathered together will help form the leaves. Extra fiber can be cut in various lengths to fill in if you think the color needs to be more opaque.

2. Continue needle felting the flower and vine design from each end of the scarf towards the center.

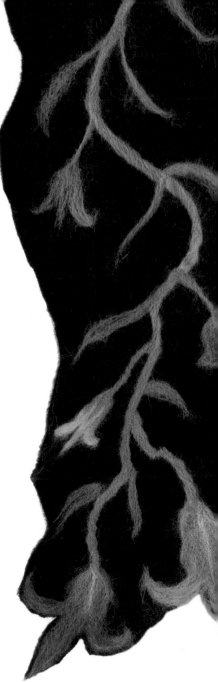

3. When design is complete and needle felting is very secure, cut around large flower designs at each end of your scarf. Cut a large scallop pattern down both sides of scarf. Scallops need not be even; your design should dictate scalloping pattern.

4. Clean stray fibers from scarf by dampening a soft cloth and lightly rubbing over scarf.

art nouveau jacket

Motifs from the past inspired the embellishment for this simple but dramatic swing jacket. Use the pattern provided or adapt the idea to your favorite jacket. Take a stroll through history or art books for inspiration...or look through books of readily available clip art to find a design that suits your taste.

Materials

- Purchase Indygo Junction's Simple Swing Jacket Pattern IJ700 or another purchased pattern with similar styling
- 2 yds. 60" wide winter white wool
- 3/4 yd. sheer, lightweight fusible interfacing
- 1/4 yd. solid or subtly printed winter white cotton for collar lining (quilting cotton weight)

- Clover natural wool roving in black
- Small scissors or craft knife
- Freezer paper or Non-Woven Water Soluble Stabilizer
- Clover felting needle tool and single felting needles
- Clover felting needle mat
- Art Nouveau design (provided in Pattern Insert)

Construction:

1. Determine the correct size. Using the pattern pieces indicated for View 2 (Simple Swing Jacket Pattern), cut the jacket front, jacket back and jacket back inset, omitting pockets and back belt. Roughly cut the collar pieces for View 2 with about 2" extra fabric all around.

2. Using the design located in the pattern insert, compare it to the jacket pattern tissue for size and make any adjustments necessary. On the matte side of the freezer paper, trace the designs for both collar pieces and the back insert. Using small scissors or a craft knife, cut the patterns out of the freezer paper, creating 3 stencils. Or use non-woven water soluble stabilizer and refer to the Needle Felting Instructions located in the Tulip Poncho project for another method to transfer the design to fabric.

Remove shaded part to create stencil

3. Using a warm, dry iron, press the freezer paper stencil, shiny side down, on the right side of fabric back inset until it adheres.

4. Using a single needle and black roving, begin to outline the pattern within the stencil. Needle felt along the stencil outline firmly. You can choose to needle felt the interior of the design lightly in place with a single needle (this helps to keep the pattern crisper, with fewer stray strands of wool, but takes a little longer) or remove the stencil once the design is outlined and use the multi-needle tool to fill in the outlines.

5. After removing the stencil, securely needle felt the entire design area and touch up any rough edges and fill in any light spots with tufts of roving. Trim any stray strands of roving that extend outside the design with small scissors.

6. Place a clean white towel on the ironing board and steam press the back inset from the wrong side. Compare the piece to the pattern tissue and gently steam and reshape if the needle felting has distorted the piece. Let dry.

7. From the interfacing, cut one jacket back inset. Position the interfacing on the wrong side of the jacket back inset. Hold the iron an inch or so above the interfacing and steam well (this takes care of any potential shrinkage in the interfacing). Fuse the interfacing to the jacket back inset according to manufacturer's instructions.

8. Place the freezer paper pattern stencil on the oversize collar pieces, aligning grain line. Using a warm, dry iron, press the freezer paper stencil, shiny side down, on the right side of fabric collar pieces.

9. Needle felt the motif on the collar pieces in the same way as the back inset (steps 4 and 5), ending needle felting at least 2" from the cutting line of the back collar for your size (the needle felting will be completed after the center back seam is sewn.)

10. Steam press the collar pieces from the wrong side.

11. Cut the collar pieces to size, carefully positioning the needle felted design as indicated on pattern piece. Using the quilting cotton, cut collar pieces for the collar lining.

12. With right sides together, stitch the center back (notched edge) of the collar. Press seam open. Repeat with the lining. Set aside. Top stitch the collar 1/4" on either side of the center back seam line.

13. Complete the needle felting on the back of the collar across the seam line. If necessary, adapt the design to form a smooth continuous design. Steam press from the wrong side.

14. Throughout jacket construction, topstitch a scant 1/4" on either side of seam lines where indicated in instructions. Follow Simple Swing Jacket pattern instructions for:

a. View 1, Step 1 & 2. If the wool that you are using does not ravel, you may omit step 1.

b. View 1, Step 4 through 7. If the wool that you are using does not ravel, you may omit step 4.

15. There are two options to finish the outside edges of the jacket and collar.

a. If the wool ravels or you prefer the appearance of a serged edge, serge the outside edges as indicated in the pattern instructions.

b. If the wool is relatively stable and does not ravel or you don't have a serger, it may be finished with a zigzag edge.

16. *If using a serged finish:* Layer the collar and collar lining wrong sides together. Serge both layers as one along the collar bottom and outside edges. *If using a zigzag edging:* On the collar lining, turn 3/8" to the wrong side on the bottom and out

side edges and press. With wrong sides together, pin the lining to the collar, matching centers and unpressed edges. From the wrong side, stitch with a short, medium width zigzag. Stitch so that the "zag" of the stitch just catches the cotton lining. From the right side, trim seam allowance cleanly as close as possible to the zigzag stitching, taking care not to cut stitches.

Stitch from wrong side just catching lining

From right side trim as close as possible to stitching without cutting threads.

17. Continue with pattern instructions for View 2, step 8 (Simple Swing Jacket Pattern), being sure to use a *generous 1/4" seam allowance.*

18. If serging all edges, continue with View 2, step 9 (Simple Swing Jacket Pattern). If you do not have a serger, substitute a medium zigzag stitch next to the straight stitching and trim close to zigzag stitching.

19. Press seam allowance toward collar. Clip to the stitching line at the bottom of the collar and press front edge under a generous 1/4". From the right side, starting at the bottom edge, topstitch a scant 1/4" from the front edge. Continue stitching under the collar close to the seam through the seam allowance, and topstitch the remaining front edge.

20. If using serged edges, continue with pattern instructions for View 2, step 11 through 13 (Simple Swing Jacket Pattern). If using zigzag stitching, stitch 1/4" from the edge and trim.

21. Steam press jacket, paying particular attention to outside edges, shrinking in any fullness.

baby bouquet sweater and hat

Approximate size: six to fifteen months. This baby jacket and hat are created from two adult sweaters. Both sweaters used were cashmere, but it can be constructed from any two sweaters of 100% wool.

Materials

- Two adult cashmere or wool sweaters. For the sample, the blue pieces originate from a men's V-neck sweater and the pink pieces are from a women's cowl neck sweater. Virtually any sweater with somewhat traditional styling and ribbing can be adapted to work with this project.
- Three buttons of varied size, new or vintage (sample uses sizes 1", 1 1/8" and 1 3/8")
- Five colors of Clover natural wool roving (sample uses teal, violet, lime green, moss green and pink)
- A small amount of green netting and pink tulle (or any colors you choose)
- Thread to match each sweater color
- Clover felting needle tool and/or single felting needles
- Clover felting needle mat

The cashmere stays incredibly soft and pliable, even after felting which is especially nice for babies. Although generally rather expensive, these were purchased at a clothing outlet for under ten dollars each. Search thrift stores, garage sales, clearance sales or the back of your own closet for sweaters to felt and restyle. Add the embellishments for a serious dose of preciousness. These make an unforgettable gift of heirloom caliber.

Felting Instructions:

To felt your sweaters, wash them in warm water and dry them on low heat. This causes the wool fibers to shrink and condense so that they do not ravel. The "denser" wool then makes a good palate for needle felting in wool roving in others fibers. You may need to wash and dry them more than once to achieve the density you desire. Don't wash and dry it too much or the garment will become too stiff and not wearable. Cashmere will stay considerably thinner and softer than traditional wool sweaters.

Pattern Pieces Needed:
• Jacket Upper Front (provided in Pattern Insert)
• Jacket Upper Back (provided in Pattern Insert)
• Jacket Sleeve (provided in Pattern Insert)
• Flower 1 (provided in Pattern Insert)
• Flower 2 (provided in Pattern Insert)
• Jacket Lower Front (instructions provided)
• Jacket Lower Back (instructions provided)

Jacket Lower Front pattern piece:
To make this simple pattern piece, follow these instructions: Use copier paper, newspaper, newsprint, etc. Using a ruler draw a rectangle 8 1/4" x 5 1/2". Draw a notch on the top long side to indicate the upper edge. Measure 1/4" to the left of the LOWER left corner and make a dot. Draw a line from this dot to the UPPER left corner. Draw a notch on this now slightly diagonal line. This will be your side edge. Write "Jacket Lower Front / Cut 2" on this pattern piece.

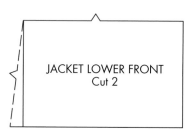

Jacket Lower Back pattern piece:
To make this pattern piece, follow these instructions: Using a ruler draw a rectangle 7 1/2" x 5 1/2". Draw a notch on the top long side to indicate the upper edge. On the LEFT short side write Place on FOLD. Measure 1/4" to the right of the LOWER right corner and make a dot. Draw a line from this dot to the UPPER right corner. This slightly diagonal line is your side cutting line. Write "Jacket Lower Back / Cut 1 on FOLD" on this pattern piece.

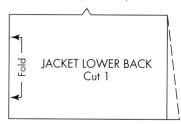

Baby Hat:
• Hat Top (provided in Pattern Insert)
• Flower 1 (provided in Pattern Insert)
• Hat Crown (instructions provided)
• Hat Brim (instructions provided)

Hat Crown pattern piece:
To make this pattern piece, follow these instructions: Using a ruler, draw a rectangle 10 13/16" x 3 7/8". On right short side write Place on FOLD. On the LEFT short side draw two notches and write Center Back Seam 5/8". On the top long edge draw a notch to indicate that it is the upper edge and write 3/8" seam allowance. Write "Hat Crown / Cut 1" on this pattern piece.

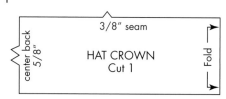

baby bouquet sweater continued

Hat Brim pattern piece:

To make this pattern piece follow these instructions: Using a ruler draw a rectangle 10 13/16" x 5 1/4". On right short side write Place on FOLD. On the LEFT short side draw two notches and write Center Back Seam 5/8". On the top long edge draw a notch to indicate that it is the upper edge and write 3/8" seam allowance. Write "Hat Brim / Cut 1" on this pattern piece.

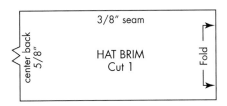

Cutting Instructions for Blue Sweater:

1. Cut off the neck ribbing, sleeve ribbing and lower edge ribbing, keeping them in one continuous length and set aside.

2. Cut off sleeves at the seam connecting sleeve to body of sweater. Cut through underarm seam of sleeves to open them out flat.

3. Cut through side seams and across shoulder seams to create two large expanses of workable fabric from the front and the back of the sweater.

4. Using both sleeve fabrics and your jacket sleeve pattern piece (provided), cut out two sleeves.

5. From the body, cut out Jacket Upper Back, two Jacket Upper Fronts, Hat Top, and Hat Crown. It may be necessary to piece together sweater sections to create the size of the pattern piece. Just use a narrow 1/4" seam.

6. Cut through the side seam of lower edge ribbing to make one long length. From one long edge measure up 1 3/4" and mark. From here cut a length that is 45 1/2" x 1 3/4" and set aside. You may need to piece this to achieve desired length. Just overlap sections slightly and stitch through center of overlapped fabric. This will be your jacket tie.

7. Cut out two Flower 1 pieces, one for jacket and one for hat.

8. From the remaining lower edge ribbing cut the left front placket, 12" x 3/4".

9. From sleeve ribbing cut two jacket sleeve trims, 9" x 3/4".

Cutting Instructions for Pink Sweater:

1. Cut off the neck ribbing and sleeve ribbing ONLY, leaving the lower edge ribbing intact.

2. Cut off sleeves at the seam, connecting sleeve to body of sweater. Cut through underarm seam of sleeves to open them out flat.

3. Cut through side seams and across shoulder seams to create two large expanses of workable fabric from the front and the back of the sweater.

4. From the main body cut out the Jacket Lower Fronts and the Jacket Lower Back. The bottom edge of these pattern pieces should be positioned along the lower edge of the sweater ribbing so that you will have this finished edge on your garment. See photograph.

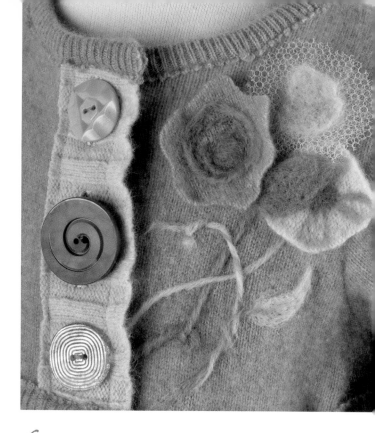

5. To make the right front placket you will need a ribbed section 12" x 1 5/8". Ribbing should be horizontal on placket. See photograph. For the sample we used the sleeve ribbing which we pieced together in the center to make the correct length. The seam is hidden beneath the tie of the jacket.

6. Cut 1 Hat Brim wherever you desire. Our sample uses a brim cut from the cowl neck.

7. Cut one Flower 1 and one Flower 2.

Assembly and Embellishment Instructions for the Jacket:

1. With right sides together, pin notched edge of Jacket Lower Fronts to lower edge of Jacket Upper Fronts. Stitch 1/4" seam allowance. Press open.

2. With right sides together, pin notched edge of Jacket Lower Back to lower edge of Jacket Upper Back. Stitch 1/4" seam allowance. Press open.

3. With right sides together, pin and stitch shoulder seams of jacket 5/8" seam allowance. Trim and press open.

4. With right sides together, pin and stitch side seams of jacket 5/8" seam allowance. Trim and press open.

5. Position right front placket (cut from pink sweater) on the right front edge so that it extends beyond edge 1/4". Align top edges of placket and jacket. Pin. Trim lower edge of placket if it extends beyond bottom of garment. Stitch in place 3/8" from right edge and a scant 1/4" from left edge. Stitch across upper and lower edges of placket between the vertical stitching.

6. On LEFT front edge, position the left front placket (cut from blue sweater) allowing placket to extend a scant 1/8" beyond front edge of garment. Align upper and lower edges of placket and jacket. Trim if necessary. Pin and stitch close to left edge from top to bottom of placket. Stitch down right side of placket just far enough to secure to the jacket beneath. Stitch across upper and lower edges of placket.

7. Press the neck ribbing that was removed from blue sweater in half lengthwise, wrong sides together to form neck binding. Beginning at right front edge of jacket, place this pressed binding over jacket neck (and front plackets) with the raw edge of neck in the fold of the binding. Pin. Trim binding as necessary so that it is flush with front edges of jacket. Stitch 1/8" from raw edge of binding being certain to catch in binding beneath.

8. Position jacket tie right side up around jacket. Upper edge of tie should be 3/4" above connecting seam of upper and lower jacket. Right front tie will extend about 9" beyond right front edge. Left front tie will extend approximately 4" beyond left front edge. Pin securely and stitch around 1/8" below upper

baby bouquet sweater

edge of tie. On RIGHT front stop stitching 3/8" from right front edge. Backstitch to secure. On LEFT front stop stitching about 6 3/4" from left front edge. Backstitch to secure.

9. Lay jacket sleeves flat, right side up. Position sleeve trim (cut from blue sweater) along lower edge so that trim extends 1/16" below edge of sleeve. Pin. Stitch close to upper edge of trim. Stitch across again 1/8" from lower edge of trim being careful to catch bottom of sleeve.

10. Baste a 5/8" seam between notches on upper sleeves. On LEFT sleeve, with right sides together, pin and stitch underarm sleeve seam using a 5/8" seam allowance. Trim and press open. Set aside.

11. Embellish the lower center of the RIGHT sleeve in the following manner:
Cut two circles of green netting, 2 1/2" diameter. Cut three circles of pink tulle, 1 3/4" diameter. Center tulle circles on netting. Place all on felting mat, tulle side DOWN. Place small amount of pink roving in center of netting and needle felt through until the opposite side is "fuzzy". Turn over – the fuzzy side will be the top of your flower. Center this on lower right sleeve. Place on felting mat and felt through center of flower to adhere to sleeve. Use some pink thread to make a few stitches through center of flower to keep intact. Use lime green and moss green roving to complete the flower stems as shown. Twist moss roving into ropes and let them meander to the left and right of flower. Felt into sleeve. Felt in a small lime roving leaf shape to the left and right of flower.

12. With right sides together, pin and stitch underarm sleeve seam using a 5/8" seam allowance. Trim and press open.

13. Turn sleeve RIGHT side out. Hold garment WRONG side out with armhole facing you. With right sides together, pin sleeve to armhole, aligning the underarm seams and the large dot at top of sleeve to shoulder seam. Pull up basting stitches to fit. Pin. Stitch in 5/8" seam.

14. Stitch three buttonholes in right front placket, evenly spaced between neck binding and jacket tie.

15. Final step – embellishment of sweater body:

a. In the center of a flower cut from blue sweater, felt a spiral of violet roving. Around the violet, felt a circle of teal roving.

b. In center of flower cut from pink sweater felt a 1/2" diameter circle of violet roving. Felt in eight lines of teal roving radiating out from it.

c. Cut out two circles of green netting 2 3/8". Cut out three 1 3/4" circles of pink tulle. Stack and center these on netting. Place all of these tulle side down, on felting mat. Felt in a circle of pink roving with a smaller piece of lime roving next to it. Felt until roving comes out "fuzzy" on the opposite side. Turn over and use this as your completed flower.

d. Form a triangle of the three flowers as seen in photograph on upper left front of jacket. Place a felting mat beneath and felt through the center of the flowers to adhere to jacket. Using a needle and thread, make a few stitches through flower centers to hold them securely.

e. Twist some long ropes of moss green and lime green roving to form stems from flower bases to left front placket. Felt into jacket front. Form a small leaf of lime green roving and add to one of the stems.

f. On your felting mat, form a moss green leaf shape. Felt with needles and add roving until a solid leaf shape can be lifted from brush. Place this under front flower and felt into jacket.

g. Continue your meandering stems starting from under right tie and having them move diagonally across lower right front, continuing past right side seam to the back of the jacket for six inches or so. Form some small loops in the roving as you work.

16. Stitch buttons to left front beneath buttonholes.

Assembly and Embellishment Instructions for the Hat:

1. With right sides together, pin and stitch double notched ends of Hat Crown 5/8" seam allowance. Press open.

2. With right sides together, pin and stitch Hat Crown to Hat Top 3/8" seam allowance. Press.

3. With right sides together, pin and stitch double notched edge of Hat Brim 5/8" seam allowance. Press open. Press under unnotched edge of hat brim 1/2".

4. With RIGHT side of brim (unfolded edge) to WRONG side of crown, align center back seams and raw edges. Pin and stitch 3/8" seam allowance. Press.

5. Fold the pressed under edge to the OUTSIDE of hat so that pressed under edge rests about 1" below seam of Hat Top. Pin and slip stitch in place so that stitching is not visible.

6. If desired, form a pleat in the hat brim just to the left of center front by folding under 1/2" of brim and stitching down by hand.

7. To embellish hat follow these instructions:

a. Embellishment will be placed just to the left of center front with or without a pleat.

b. Through centers of your two remaining flowers, felt lines of violet and teal roving. Roll in the bottoms of each flower and slip stitch the lower half to secure. See photograph.

c. Cut two circles of green netting and three smaller circles of pink tulle. Center tulle circles on netting circles and place tulle side down on felting mat. Felt through the center a circle of pink roving and a small amount of lime roving until it comes through "fuzzy" on the opposite side. This flower will serve as the center of your hat embellishment. Felt into hat with needles. Add stitching to center to secure completely. Hand stitch the wool flowers to the right and left of this center flower.

d. Directly on hat, felt a rope of moss green roving out from the left flower. Let it trail for about 5 or 6 inches. On your felting mat make a leaf shape of lime green roving. Continue to add roving and felt it until you have a solid shape that can be lifted from the mat. Felt into bottom of left flower. Use stitches to secure if necessary.

swirl girl child's coat

This project creates a unique and toasty toddler-sized coat, approximately a size 3/4 by felting an adult-size small crewneck sweater. Using an adult-size medium to create a cardigan for a somewhat older child. The entire project is created by hand, except for the machine stitched buttonholes, and requires only basic sewing skills. The embellishments are easy to recreate. Rich jewel tone fabrics, roving and yarn lends visual delight while the quirky styling and embellishments add a note of fun for children.

Materials

- One 100% wool adult-size small crewneck sweater
- Three colors of wool or wool blend yarn (sample uses violet, brown, and teal)
- Two colors of Clover wool roving (sample uses teal and violet)

- Four small pieces of wool for tabs (sample uses Weeks Dye Works turquoise houndstooth, violet houndstooth, teal herringbone, and rose houndstooth.
- You will also need 1/2 yard wool for front and sleeve bindings (sample uses Weeks Dye Works brown herringbone)

Materials *continued*

- A variety of embroidery floss colors to match or contrast as you desire (sample uses Weeks Dye Works floss in lavender, turquoise, aqua, moss and brown)
- Sewing thread colors to match or contrast as you desire (samples uses brown, moss green and turquoise)
- Four mismatched buttons in interesting shapes (sample buttons range in size from 1 3/8" to 2 1/4"
- Sewing needle with hole large enough for three strands of embroidery floss
- Pinking sheers (optional). Directions will be given with pinking sheers but you may use regular scissors instead
- Clover felting needle tool and/or single felting needle
- Clover felting needle mat

Felting Instructions:

Wash your sweater in warm water and dry on low heat. This will significantly shrink your sweater and condense the fibers so that it no longer ravels when cut. Sometimes it is necessary to repeat this procedure to achieve the desired "density". The condensed fibers make a good palate for felting in wool roving and other fibers. Don't felt too much or your wool will become too stiff to wear comfortably.

Pattern Pieces Needed:

Pattern pieces are located in Pattern Insert.
- Tab 1, cut from turquoise houndstooth
- Tab 2, cut from violet houndstooth
- Tab 3, cut from teal herringbone
- Tab 4, cut from rose houndstooth
- Right front felting guideline

Cutting Instructions:

1. Lay sweater flat, with the front right side up and measure with ruler across chest. Determine center front and mark. Cut sweater vertically from top to bottom through this mark.

2. Lay sleeves flat on table. Beginning where sleeve underarm is connected to body of sweater, measure down 10" along underarm seam and mark. Cut straight across sleeve at this point (parallel with sleeve binding). SAVE LOWER SLEEVE SECTIONS.

Assembly and Embellishment Instructions:

1. To create your front bindings measure the vertical length of sweater front edges, from bottom of neck ribbing to bottom edge of the sweater. Cut two lengths of wool the same vertical length by 1 1/2" wide from the front and sleeve binding wool. Pink the long edges if desired. With wrong sides together, press in half lengthwise. Place one of these bindings over right front edge, starting at the bottom of the sweater's neck ribbing and position raw edge of sweater inside crease of binding. Pin. (If necessary, trim excess binding at bottom of sweater.) With three strands of embroidery floss (color: aqua) hand sew a running stitch through all three thicknesses from top to bottom of binding about 1/8" in from pinked edge. Repeat procedure on left front edge.

2. Fold neck ribbing of sweater in half to OUTSIDE. Pin. Using three strands of embroidery floss (color: brown) hand sew a running stitch around perimeter of neck close to folded down edge.

3. With a seam ripper or scissors, remove stitching from underarm seam for about 2 1/2" up from lower cut edge. Reinforce stitching of underarm seam at this point, if necessary. Lay lower edge of sleeve as flat as possible and measure width of lower edge. From the front and sleeve binding wool, cut two pieces of wool this length by 1 1/4" wide. These will serve as your sleeve bindings. Pink the long edges of binding, if desired. With wrong sides together, press in half lengthwise. Place one of these bindings over the right sleeve edge, positioning raw edge of sleeve in pressed crease of binding. Pin. (If necessary, trim excess binding at edge) With three strands embroidery floss (color: lavender), hand sew a running stitch close to pinked edge through all thicknesses to secure binding to sleeve. Repeat on left sleeve.

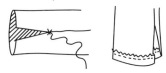

4. Turn up lower right sleeve where underarm stitching ceases, to form a cuff. On wrong side of sweater around this upturned cuff, just under the binding, felt in six circles of wool roving (color: teal) that are approximately 1/2" in diameter. Repeat on left cuff.

5. Open the underarm seams on the lower sleeve sections that were cut off in Step 2 of the Cutting Instructions. Lay flat. You will use these to construct pockets.

6. Turn one section so that ribbing is on top. This will be the top of Pocket 1. Trim so that the width of the pocket measures 6" and the height measures 4 1/2". Pink sides and lower edge of pocket. Felt five, 1/2" diameter circles of wool roving (color: teal) across top of pocket about 1/4" below top ribbing edge.

Pocket 1

7. Unwind a length of wool yarn (color: violet). Do not cut until pattern is completed. Lay pocket on felting mat. Beginning at lower right corner, tack in yarn straight across pocket and around to form pattern shown. Cut yarn when design is achieved and felted securely in place with multi-needle tool or single felting needle.

8. Position pocket on lower right front of coat, about 1" above lower edge and pin so that pocket wraps to back of coat over side seam an inch or so. Using three strands of contrasting embroidery floss (color: turquoise) hand sew a tight running stitch down both sides and across lower edge of pocket to secure to coat.

Run yarn back and forth over pocket so that yarn extends BEYOND side edges about 3/8". Continue to lower edge of pocket.

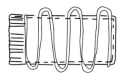

11. Pin this pocket, right side up, centered on upper left sleeve. This is a little awkward but not too difficult with such a small garment. With three strands of embroidery floss (color: Brown) hand sew a running stitch down sides and across lower edge to secure pocket to sleeve, being careful not to sew sleeve together.

12. Place remaining Pocket 3 on felting mat with ribbing on top. Across the top felt three to five 1/2" diameter circles with wool roving (color: violet). They should be about 1/4" below top edge. Across the lower portion of the pocket needle felt three undulating lines of wool yarn (color: brown).

13. Position this completed pocket on right front of garment just above the first pocket. Pin. With three strands of embroidery floss (color: brown) hand sew a running stitch to secure pocket to coat along sides and lower edge. Set aside.

14. With wrong sides together, fold wool tabs in half along fold line. Pull top half slightly back so that lower half extends just a bit beyond upper half. On Tabs 2 and 4, pink unfolded edges if desired. Pin. On Tabs 1, 2 and 4 use three strands embroidery floss to hand sew a running stitch through both thicknesses around unfolded edges to connect them, about 1/8" from edges. Tab 1 uses Brown floss, Tab 2 uses Turquoise floss and Tab 4 uses moss floss.

9. Turn remaining lower sleeve section (seam removed) so that ribbing is on top. From one side edge, measure over 2 5/8" and cut straight down from top to bottom to form left sleeve Pocket 2 (approximately 2 5/8" wide x 4 1/2" high). Pink sides and lower edge of this narrow pocket. From remainder of sleeve section, cut another pocket (with ribbing on top) that is approximately 3" tall. Any width is fine. This will depend on your individual sweater. Pink sides and lower edge. Set aside.

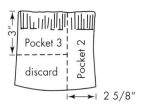

10. To embellish left sleeve Pocket 2, unroll a length of wool yarn (color: teal), but do not cut until pattern is complete. Place sleeve pocket on felting mat. Begin needle felting just under upper ribbing.

swirl girl child's coat continued

On Tab 3 hand sew a running stitch with three strands floss down the long sides, but across the end make four X's with your floss to connect upper and lower halves of tab. Tab 3 uses aqua floss. Stitch buttonholes in tabs using markings on pattern pieces. Adjust for the size of your buttons.

15. Place folded edge of Tab 1 - 7/8" under right front binding edge of garment just below neck binding. Pin. Using a single strand of sewing thread (color: turquoise), hand sew five vertical rows of a running stitch through front binding to secure tab to coat.

16. Place folded edge of Tab 2 - 7/8" under right front binding edge of garment 3/4" below first tab. Pin. Using a single strand of sewing thread (color: moss green) hand sew eight horizontal rows of a running stitch through front binding to secure tab to coat.

17. Position folded edge of Tab 3 ON TOP of right front binding edge of garment beginning 3/4" below Tab 2. Pin. Using a single strand of sewing thread (color: brown) hand sew five vertical rows of a running stitch through front binding to secure tab to coat.

18. Place folded edge of Tab 4 - 7/8" under right front binding edge of garment beginning 3/4" below Tab 3. Pin. Using a single strand of sewing thread (color: moss green) hand sew four large X's vertically through front binding to secure tab to coat.

19. Stitch buttons to left front of coat beneath buttonholes.

20. Use the "Right Front Felting Guideline" provided to needle felt wool yarn (color: violet) to right front of garment. You may simply use it as a visual aid or you may transfer to garment using a transfer pencil. Place felting mat under right front and tack yarn into place. Have it descend slightly into upper pocket. Cut yarn when design is achieved. Thoroughly felt into coat.

21. Unroll a length of wool yarn (color: violet), place lower left front of coat on felting mat and begin looping yarn starting at front binding up 1" from lower edge of coat. Make loops ranging in size from 1" to 2" in height. Just sort of let the yarn fall where it will. This makes an interesting pattern. Continue around back of coat stopping at right side seam. Tack in place with single needle. When you are satisfied with pattern, needle felt yarn securely with multi needle tool or single felting needle.

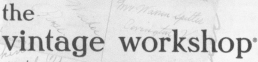